THE LAUREL POETRY SERIES *is unique
in the growing range of fine, inexpensive
paperbound books. Each volume
contains the works of a single poet,
along with an original introduction,
a chronology of the poet's career, a
bibliography and notes on the poetry.*

JOHN MALCOLM BRINNIN *is the author
of six books of verse, the latest
called "Skin Diving in the Virgins".
His biographical study of Gertrude Stein,
"The Third Rose", has been highly praised.
Mr. Brinnin now teaches at
Boston University.*

RICHARD WILBUR, *the General Editor,
has won the Pulitzer Prize, the
National Book Award, and the Millay
Prize, all three in 1957 for his book of
poems, "Things of This World." His
most recent volume of poetry is "Walking
to Sleep." Professor Wilbur has
held a Guggenheim and a Prix de Rome
Fellowship, and is a member of the
National Institute of Arts and Letters.
He is now Professor of English at
Wesleyan University.*

The Laurel Poetry Series
General Editor, Richard Wilbur

Emily
Dickinson

Selected, with an
introduction and notes,
by John Malcolm Brinnin

Published by
DELL PUBLISHING CO., INC.
1 Dag Hammarskjold Plaza
New York, N.Y. 10017

Laurel ® TM 674623, Dell Publishing Co., Inc.

ISBN: 0-440-32304-5

Typography by Alvin Eisenman

Cover drawing by Richard Powers

First printing: September, 1960
Second printing: April, 1961
Third printing: April, 1963
Fourth printing: April, 1964
Fifth printing: October, 1964
Sixth printing: September, 1965
Seventh printing: March, 1966
Eighth printing: March, 1967
Ninth printing: November, 1967
Tenth printing: October, 1968
Eleventh printing: October, 1969
Twelfth printing: January, 1970
Thirteenth printing: May, 1971
Fourteenth printing: June, 1972
Fifteenth printing: July, 1973
Sixteenth printing: October, 1974
Seventeenth printing: March 1976
Eighteenth printing: February, 1977
Nineteenth printing: January 1978
Twentieth printing: June 1979

Printed in U.S.A.

Contents

Emily Dickinson, The Legend and the Poet

Although her stature in American letters is great, Emily Dickinson's story is uncommonly barren of events and modest in pretensions. The example of her life has nevertheless made her one of the saints of art and one of the eponymous legends of national history.

In the popular sense, achievement in art is generally recognized by mass acceptance, worldly rewards and the indiscriminate homage given to artists who become "names." Yet people who ordinarily understand success by these tokens are moved and delighted by the story of genius fashioning its signature in silence and obscurity. Emily Dickinson, like her contemporaries, Alfred Pinkham Ryder and Herman Melville, was flushed out of the thickets of obscurity in which she lived and acclaimed a figure of honor long after most of the publicly successful artists of her time were forgotten. Like her, both Ryder and Melville were discovered and for the first time "understood" and taken to heart by the generations that came after them. But the austere dedication of these men to their respective arts satisfied only part of the demands of legend. In the case of Emily Dickinson, romantic renunciation humanized the austerity of the record; and a doughty spirit asserting itself over religion and society alike made her story heroic.

Her poems tell it all, and what they say should be the final truth. But legend, unscrupulous of truth, tends to shape itself in the image of its makers rather than in the image of its subjects. Now, less than seventy-five years after her death, the legend of Emily Dickinson has congealed into a shape not even the poems themselves seem

7

able seriously to disturb. It takes its character mainly from the romantic sorrows of a vivacious, witty young woman of distinguished family who fell in love, suffered rejection, and spent the remainder of her life in a white solitude that was, in the words of her finest biographer, George Frisbie Whicher, "a long interval of sameness so absolute that the arrival of a new month was like a guest's coming and the closed vans of a circus passing her window at night seemed to her an Arabian experience." When Emily Dickinson became the nun in the cloisters of her father's house, enacting in her poems the bittersweet resignation of thwarted love and accepting marriage to nothing but the universe, she had unconsciously made a place for herself among the tragic heroines of drama and fiction. Her story has the necessary elements that make for legend—love at once and for all time, love as sacrifice —and she possessed the genius to transform a private circumstance into one of general relevance. When she chose to confirm her fate by dressing in the costume of a perpetual bride, she gave legend an enduring image; and when she confided her secret in a privacy that, long after her death, her poems would destroy, she added the proper touch of irony that would complete the picture.

Legend has a way of flourishing in proportion to its degree of falsehood. Biographical scrutiny has never certified the man or men whom legend has accepted as the variously possible objects of her love, and there is good reason—on the basis of her poems as well as her recorded friendships—to believe that her emotional life was more deeply attuned to feminine attachments. Wherever the biographic truth may lie, the young poet whose personal romance grew into the famous romance of the life of Emily Dickinson is a portrait drawn from but one side of her character, one area of her living interests. The histrionic bias of the myth-makers, and the tendency of others to make a darling of an artist the world abused by ignoring, have been in effect joined in a cabal that stands somewhere between the poet and her poems. Beyond the single figure of the legend, there are several strong and

8

distinct Emily Dickinsons. Each of the several versions of her character is amply documented in her poems. Phase by phase, they succeed merely in putting strictures upon the legend they will probably never demolish.

Perhaps the least accountable to the public eye is the Emily Dickinson who can speak with the unassuageable fury of a Medea—the blunt, self-exacerbating woman whose grief makes her grotesque:

> Title divine is mine
> The Wife without
> The Sign.
> Acute degree
> Conferred on me—
> Empress of Calvary.
> Royal all but the
> Crown—
> Betrothed, without the swoon
> God gives us women
> When two hold
> Garnet to garnet,
> Gold to gold—
> Born—Bridalled—
> Shrouded—
> In a day
> Tri-Victory—
> "My Husband"
> Women say
> Stroking the melody,
> Is this the way?

This is a document so stark it seems less to have been composed with a pencil on paper than to have been cut with hatchet-strokes. The bitterness packed into its last lines and the mad smile that seems to hover over its conclusion are not common elements in her work, yet they signify a tendency to distortion widely manifest in her poems, most of which are governed by milder measures and conform to less dissonant expressions of pathos. The modern critical commonplace of "tragic acceptance" does

9

not easily apply to the persistently disconsolate mind of Emily Dickinson, but in the many instances where she subjects personal chaos to composition the term becomes relevant. Her art is primarily one of economy and control, and in glimpses like this we learn *what* she controlled and thereby gain insight into the denials and exclusions that shaped her verse no less rigorously than her life. Many of her finest works have the quality of outrage packed into formal dispositions of words and all but stifled in the process. In these instances we read the comparatively sane statements of a spirit half-surrendered to madness, a celebrant of the "gay, ghastly, holiday" where "terror's free," where

> The possibility to pass
> Without a moment's bell,
> Into Conjecture's presence—
> Is like a face of steel

> That suddenly looks into ours
> With a metallic grin—
> The cordiality of Death
> Who drills his welcome in.

Her legend does not conveniently accommodate the out-size "Empress of Calvary" whose suffering goads her to defy the very God her deeper nature wants only to praise for His every manifestation of "the daily miracle." Neither does it find room for the defeated woman who, with careful malevolence, undermines the divine optimism that promises her only salvation. In this role she is never the pretty versifier or the sprightly caroler of the New England idyll or even the long-suffering communicant with nature. In this role she is the demonic artist in fury, wrenching the tight meters and neat figures of her characteristic language in order to come upon utterance adequate to her anguish.

A second Emily Dickinson is the reclusive bride of silence—the radiant girl in white who tarries in the world like an ethereal visitor and associates on speaking terms with birds, bees, butterflies, lilacs and gentians as her only equals. She is the one for whom isolation from society is the way to grace—a discipline that involves the universe. She is the one for whom the unknowable is as present to her vision as the view from her window. Since her covenants with Time, Death and Immortality are real, she is able to look down upon the small events of life with the grand indulgence of those who feel themselves of the elect. Her theme in this role is imminence—the imminence of Death and Revelation—and in a hundred expressions she dramatizes the breath of God on her hand and the tug of eternity in her bones. As her denial of ordinary life approaches the absolute, her embrace of the universe becomes all but final. This is the strongest Emily Dickinson and the most pliable. Her mind plays like lightning between the immediate and the ultimate. To her, a fire in a neighbor's barn is not merely a local disaster to which she responds with natural sympathy; it is also the fire that burns Rome and the flames that gut the great library at Alexandria; finally it is the idea of fire as the destructive element itself. This is Emily Dickinson in possession of her affections and, at the same time, conversant with the human fate that primordially dooms them. When she writes her address, she puts down Main Street, Amherst, Massachusetts, but she means The Mind of God.

Emily Dickinson the dutiful daughter, affectionate sister and compassionate neighbor is another of the figures that emerge from her poetry and is perhaps the most generally engaging one. Since she was not taken up with the world's affairs—even to the extent that they were carried on amid the academic quiet of her town—she was not subject to mundane responsibilities and was subsequently above praise or blame. A citizen among her townsmen yet not subject to the rules by which they lived, she became a sort of hovering presence, the ornamental eccentric of a community independent enough to harbor her with as much pride as embarrassment. "For the last fifteen years of her life," according to George Frisbie Whicher, "the village knew Emily Dickinson only as a white figure flitting about the garden in the summer dusk, as a voice from the dimness of the hall startling visitors in the Dickinson parlor by spectral interjections, or as a presence responding to occasion for congratulation or condolence by neighborly gifts of flowers and dainties accompanied by little notes pencilled in an odd hand and phrased in orphic idiom." In spite of her isolation, she was solicitous of village life, held it closely in her attention long after she had ceased to be part of it, and observed it constantly from behind the curtains of her window and the hedges of her garden. Her poems show in abundance her affection for men, women and children. While this feeling was real, her own sense of necessity kept it distant from its objects except on the many occasions when death provoked her elegies. Death was always larger to her than life, and not until she saw a beloved neighbor in its perspective was his individual meaning apt to command her full attention. The shy spirit of her own household and of the next-door residence of her brother and his wife, she was even in these places the removed observer. Human sympathies engaged her deeply but, holding herself free to her own commitments, she found her own plateau of vantage. From this elevation she played a game of conceits with the cosmos. Matters of Calvinist sermons that her townsmen might mull over on their way home from church, news of war, and reports from abroad appearing in the *Springfield Daily Republican*, all became part of the philosophic reaches of her solitary communion. She tamed them to her hand, domesticated them, turned them out in neatly dressed stanzas and then in most cases put them away like dolls for which she had no further use.

The final, and the least memorable of the several Emily Dickinsons is, unfortunately, perhaps the one most widely quoted. This Emily Dickinson is the writer of verses as quaintly flowered and full of jingles as a rack of greeting cards. She is the coy Emily who holds to an eternally protracted girlhood, whose childish postures have never been outgrown, who assumes the histrionic or culturally pious attitudes of her time and who flirts with all the creatures of the earth and air as if she were the inhabitant of a nineteenth-century Disneyland. This is the Emily Dickinson who makes God "a noted clergyman," who reduces the figures of history and literature to the plaster bathos of the Rogers Group, and whose maidenish tolerance of drunkenness and other kinds of misbehavior in the big world makes a sophisticated reader writhe with discomfort. In the poems selected for this book, the version of Emily Dickinson's character least represented is the saucy little rebel in God's back yard who teases words into the shapes of rococo valentines.

Psychology may hold clues to great disparities among aspects of Emily Dickinson's personality, but only her poetry provides the evidence that forces us to read her "letter to the world." Whatever emotional disaster it was that drove her to elect and finally to covet a life of obscurity, poetry was the thing that made that life tolerable and transformed it into a creative career. Poetry was her trade, and with a master hand she carried it on in the same Yankee devotion to design and craft that produced the beautiful New England artifacts of silver, glass and wood, and the matchless Clipper ships. When her hand was attuned to her spirit, she worked in the harmony of genius that makes its own world and produces things of absolute individuality. Emily Dickinson's intelligence was double-edged, too sharp to accept the religion of her generation without making private rejections orthodoxy would not countenance, and altogether too great to be confined within the limits of the fastidiously genteel education to which proper young women of her day were subjected. She gave dogma no quarter—refusing to accept the idea of original sin or the belief that Christ was her redeemer. The Bible was a territory of myth that she loved, but the strictures upon behavior educed from it by believers were not those she could adopt. Her imagination, released by personal discipline and strengthened

13

by vicissitude, was too lively to accept revealed religion and too restless to abide in the world comfortably defined by the popular science and philosophy of the nineteenth century. At first an instrument of escape from such confinements, poetry eventually became for her the means of accession to a state where intimations of immortality became daily thoughts registered as daily tasks.

But her kind of domestic mysticism would have gone for little in the world's eye had she not from her early years shown that she possessed that angelic familiarity with language that defines the poet. The vast collection of manuscripts she left behind prove that she turned phrases with the care of a jeweler, and that in the process of cutting, shaping and holding facets up to the light, she was no less meticulous or adept. Her poems, for the most part, are miniatures; yet the best of them fit a macrocosm into microscopic structures. Technically, her range is modest, based on the hymn-meters she knew from church and school: Common Meter, with its alternating eight and six syllables to the iambic line; Long Meter, with its eight syllables to the line; Short Meter, two lines of six syllables, followed by one of eight, then one of six; as well as the lines made up of trochaic and dactylic meters of a similar rigidity and simplicity of stanzaic design. Especially in her handling of short iambic lines, she often lacks the minimal resourcefulness that far lesser poets demonstrate with ease. Hundreds of the more than seventeen hundred poems that she wrote are rendered negligible by the overpowering monotony that insufficiently varied meters can produce. Her electric facility with a phrase and the dramatic economy of her poetic attack are nevertheless so great that hundreds of other poems are saved by way of compensation. She saw "New Englandly," and she spoke "to the point" with the concision, directness and laconic cadences of the people of her region and with their gift for making covert utterances carry more weight than the words that make them up.

When her personal rhythm is most alive, meter bends to her accent with a naturalness that all but dissolves the artifice of her simple patterns. Her use of rhyme—half-rhyme, off-rhyme, slant-rhyme, imperfect-rhyme, or whatever term is given to rhymes that do not precisely echo—has dismayed or puzzled many readers and critics who feel that the practice has caused her work to seem marred, unfinished or amateurishly awkward. In the years since her death this practice has come to seem less strange simply because many modern poets have quite casually followed her example. Expansion of the possibilities of rhyme was of great advantage to her densely packed compositions. Her breaking with convention in this respect was dictated by a sense of rightness that amounted to the bravado of genius. If her daring was the cause of many failures, more importantly it was the element in her approach to poetry that made her successes not merely self-justifying in the body of her own work but brilliant new additions to the history of English verse. These were the occasions when the solitary apprentice to form became the mistress of language, bending language to her will rather than conforming to its conventions. In view of the scores of her poems that make their impact before their rhyming unorthodoxy is perceived, it is hardly tenable, as some critics have felt, that her odd rhymes are the consequence of anything so simple as an imperfect ear.

At the time of her death in 1886, hundreds of poems were left in the hands of her sister, Lavinia, and her sister-in-law, Susan Dickinson. These women were at odds with one another, and within a few years Lavinia was at odds with Mabel Loomis Todd to whom, after Emily's death, she had assigned the task of transcribing and editing her first collection, and who had subsequently been mainly responsible for seeing it through the press. When Lavinia brought suit to recover a piece of real estate which her brother, Austin, with her consent, had

15

willed to Mrs. Todd, partly in recognition of services to Emily's literary estate, the result was a palpably unfair verdict in favor of Lavinia. Mrs. Todd, shocked by the lawsuit and dismayed by the verdict, withdrew from any further connection with the Dickinson estate, and the great bulk of the poems was left in neglect. Lavinia Dickinson who could not, unaided, prepare them for publication herself, was reluctant to allow anyone else to do so; and Susan Dickinson, for reasons of her own, preferred to withhold those in her possession. After Susan Dickinson's death, her daughter, Martha Dickinson Bianchi, began to edit and to publish the hoarded manuscripts and to dole them out to the public in a series of editions that served to increase the number of Emily Dickinson's readers but also to make them wonder when, if ever, the process of "discovery" would end. In 1945, when Mrs. Todd's daughter published the nearly seven hundred poems that her mother had transcribed more than fifty years before and which had remained in her possession, surviving a warehouse fire and the great Florida hurricane of 1926, the major part of the poet's work was finally available. But contention was not in effect dissolved until the deaths of the various parties concerned allowed the transfer of the literary estate from private hands to the Harvard College Library. In 1955, when Thomas H. Johnson published his three-volume edition of *The Poems of Emily Dickinson,* it was at last possible to assess the whole career of the poet with certainty and finality. Before Johnson's collection appeared, the two main editions generally available were the gradually accumulated *Poems of Emily Dickinson* edited by her niece, Martha Dickinson Bianchi, and Alfred Leete Hampson, and *Bolts of Melody* edited by Mabel Loomis Todd and her daughter, Millicent Todd Bingham. In the nature of the case— where private persons asserted priority to a body of literature that would seem by larger right to be part of a national heritage—rumors had long been abroad that such works of Emily Dickinson's as had been offered to the public had been tampered with, doctored, or otherwise altered to the comparatively minor poetic capacities of their respective editors. Since these rumors had beclouded the reception of the poems for many years, the publication of the Johnson volumes was awaited with great interest. But when they finally appeared, it became clear that the earlier editors of Emily Dickinson had been widely maligned. The documentations of Johnson provide a definitive source of the poems as Emily Dickinson wrote them, and yet it became obvious that, as Emily Dickinson wrote them, they would have engaged the interest of the reading public to a far lesser degree than in the form in which they had been earlier presented.

Here, for example, is one of Emily Dickinson's most famous poems, "The soul selects her own society," which appears in Volume One of Johnson's edition as follows:

> The Soul selects her own Society—
> Then—shuts the Door—
> To her divine Majority—
> Present no more—
>
> Unmoved—she notes the Chariots—pausing—
> At her low Gate—
> Unmoved—an Emperor be kneeling
> Upon her Mat—
>
> I've known her—from an ample nation—
> Choose One—
> Then—close the Valves of her attention—
> Like Stone—

For this reading Emily Dickinson herself suggested several alterations: in line 3, *On* for *To;* in line 4, *Obtrude* for *Present;* in line 8, *On (her) Rush Mat* for *Upon her Mat;* in line 11, *lids* for *Valves.* When the poem was first published in 1890 in the collection edited by Mabel Loomis Todd and Thomas Wentworth Higginson the text, including alterations of *Chariots* to *chariot's* and *be* to *is,* appeared as follows:

The soul selects her own society,
Then shuts the door;
On her divine majority
Obtrude no more.

Unmoved, she notes the chariot's pausing
At her low gate;
Unmoved, an emperor is kneeling
Upon her mat.

I've known her from an ample nation
Choose one;
Then close the valves of her attention
Like stone.

The rougher versions of Emily Dickinson's poems, the fair copies that she gathered into fascicles, allow insights into her "uncorrected" genius, and these have a value peculiar to themselves. But notably little has been lost in the transcriptions of her principal editors, Mrs. Todd and Mrs. Bianchi and, especially under the keen eye of Mrs. Todd, much in the way of clarity, appositeness and visual felicity has been gained.

Emily Dickinson seems often to be caught by conventions of prosody or to have relaxed into them, and often she seems merely to echo thoughts that reflect the safe, worn attitudes to Nature, Society or Human Woe that were the nineteenth century's particular poetic counters. Even her admirers must admit that much of her work is almost indistinguishable from the "ladies' verse" that cluttered the journals of her time. Perhaps no other major poet in America or elsewhere has written so many reams of maudlin bad verse. Although her self-critical faculty seems to be one of the least informed of her talents, it was at least always active. Since she had no mentor worthy of her caliber, no one who might have sharpened her critical sense or affirmed her importance among her contemporaries, she worked unaided by advice, approval or anything but her own minute-to-minute sense of necessity and fitness. In the long view, her talent proved to be bigger than the constraints of circumstance in which it had to function. If she is not the greatest woman poet, it is difficult, beyond the ancient praise that seals Sappho in the classic pantheon, to say who is. Her contemporaries, Elizabeth Barrett Browning and Christina Rossetti, left no body of work to match hers at its greatest and, in the twentieth century, among poets writing in English, only Marianne Moore and Elizabeth Bishop have shown themselves to be of an excellence next to hers.

Emily Dickinson belongs in the metaphysical seam of American poetry that has always been apparent behind, below and often above the more bold and far more publicly engaged utterances of Emerson and Whitman. Until the twentieth century, she has been the greatest exponent of poetry as an art of intelligence, wit and controlled emotion rather than as an index to the homilies of religious and political thought. Her posthumous appearance and her fame, in spite of the strange hazards her literary remains had to survive, bear the stamp of poetic justice. Her most celebrated contemporary, Walt Whitman, spent his years cataloguing the New World and wrapping its millions in his undiscriminating embrace. Emily Dickinson, who knew of him only in the report of someone who told her he was "disgraceful," neither catalogued the great world nor raised her voice to win its attention. Instead, she quietly discriminated, and thereby defined, a type of consciousness which was a part of the character of the New World equally as valid and as necessary as Whitman's. America held them both in the same time, if not in the same view—a circumstance in which Emily Dickinson, like the lowly rodent in one of her poems, was "the concisest tenant." Somewhere in the broad reaches of Whitman's democratic vistas, she existed wholly unto herself and, as time would prove, made the circumstance "lawful as equilibrium."

JOHN MALCOM BRINNIN
September, 1960

SELECTIVE BIBLIOGRAPHY

Editions of the poems:

The Poems of Emily Dickinson, including variant readings critically compared with all known manuscripts, edited by Thomas H. Johnson, 3 vols. (Cambridge, Massachusetts, 1955.)

The Poems of Emily Dickinson, edited by Martha Dickinson Bianchi and Alfred Leete Hampson. Introduction by Alfred Leete Hampson. (Boston, 1937.)

Bolts of Melody, New Poems of Emily Dickinson, edited by Mabel Loomis Todd and Milicent Todd Bingham. (New York, 1945.)

Letters:

The Letters of Emily Dickinson, edited by Thomas H. Johnson, 3 vols. (Cambridge, Massachusetts, 1958.)

Biography:

Bianchi, Martha Dickinson. *Emily Dickinson Face to Face, Unpublished Letters with Notes and Reminiscences.* (Boston, 1932.)

Bingham, Mabel Todd. *Ancestors' Brocades, The Literary Debut of Emily Dickinson.* (New York, 1945.)

Johnson, Thomas H. *Emily Dickinson, An Interpretive Biography.* (Cambridge, Massachusetts, 1955.)

Patterson, Rebecca. *The Riddle of Emily Dickinson.* (Boston, 1951.)

Pollitt, Josephine. *Emily Dickinson: The Human Background of Her Poetry.* (New York, 1930.)

Taggard, Genevieve. *The Life and Mind of Emily Dickinson.* (New York, 1930.)

Whicher, George Frisbie. *This Was A Poet: A Critical Biography of Emily Dickinson.* (New York, 1938.)

Criticism:

Blackmur, Richard P. "Emily Dickinson: Notes on Prejudice and Fact," *The Expense of Greatness* (1940), 106-138.

Matthiessen, F. O. "The Problem of the Private Poet," *Kenyon Review,* VII (1945), 584-597.

Tate, Allen. "Emily Dickinson," *On the Limits of Poetry* (1948), 197-213.

Wells, Henry W. *Introduction to Emily Dickinson.* (Chicago, 1947.)

Winters, Yvor. "Emily Dickinson and the Limits of Judgment," *Maule's Curse* (1938), 149-168.

Zabel, Morton D. "Christina Rossetti and Emily Dickinson," *Poetry,* 37 (1931), 213-216.

Chronology

1828 Marriage of Edward Dickinson of Amherst, Massachusetts, to Emily Norcross of Monson, Massachusetts, May 6.

1829 William Austin Dickinson born, April 16.

1830 Emily Dickinson born, December 10.

1833 Lavinia Dickinson born, February 28.

1840 The Dickinson family moved from their Main Street homestead to a house on Pleasant Street.
Portraits of the three Dickinson children, and of their parents, painted by O. A. Bullard.

1844 Emily visited relatives in Boston, Cambridge, Worcester in May and June.

1846 Emily made a four weeks' visit to Boston, late August.

1847 Emily graduated from the Amherst Academy.

1847–1848 Emily attended Mount Holyoke Female Seminary in South Hadley, Massachusetts.

1850 First publication—a valentine in prose in *The Indicator*, Amherst College undergraduate magazine.

1851 With Lavinia, Emily went to Boston for a brief visit.

1852 Publication of her first poem, "Sic transit gloria mundi," entitled, "A Valentine," in the *Springfield Daily Republican*, February 20.
Edward Dickinson became Whig Representative in the U. S. Congress.

1854 With her father and sister, Emily visited Washington and Philadelphia in April and May.

1855 The Dickinson family moved from Pleasant Street back to the homestead on Main Street, October 29.

1856 Austin Dickinson married Susan Gilbert in Geneva, New York, July 1.

1857 Emily's bread won a prize at the annual Cattle Show.

1858 Emily served as a judge in the Bread Division of the Cattle Show.

1861 The Civil War began, April.
"I taste a liquor never brewed" published under the title, "The May-Wine," in the *Springfield Daily Republican,* May 4.

1862 "Safe in their alabaster chambers" published under the title, "The Sleeping," in the *Springfield Daily Republican,* March 1.
Emily wrote to Thomas Wentworth Higginson asking his counsel in regard to her poetry, April 15.

1864 With Lavinia, Emily went to Boston for an eye examination in February.
"Some keep the Sabbath going to church" published under the title, "My Sabbath," in *The Round Table,* March 12.
"Blazing in gold and quenching in purple" published under the title, "Sunset," in the *Springfield Daily Republican,* March 30.
On a second visit to Boston for eye treatment she stayed with her nieces in Cambridge in April.

1866 "A narrow fellow in the grass" published under the title, "The Snake," in the *Springfield Daily Republican,* February 14.
Emily's niece, Martha Gilbert Dickinson, born, November 30.

1870 Thomas Wentworth Higginson visited Emily, August 16.

1873 The second and last visit of Higginson, December 3.

1874 Death of Emily's father in the Tremont House, Boston, June 16.

1875 Emily's mother suffered paralysis; Emily became her nurse.
Emily's nephew, Thomas Gilbert Dickinson, born, August 1.

1876 Helen Hunt Jackson visited Emily, October 10.

1878 A second visit by Helen Hunt Jackson in the company of her husband, October 24.
"Success is counted sweetest" published under the title, "Success," in *A Masque of Poets*, November.

1882 Emily's mother died, November 14.

1883 Her nephew, Thomas Gilbert, died, October 5.

1884 Emily suffered a nervous collapse, June 14.

1885 Helen Hunt Jackson died, August 12.
Emily's illness, diagnosed as nephritis, became severe in November.

1886 Death of Emily Dickinson, May 15.

1890 *Poems by Emily Dickinson*, First Series, published November 12.

1891 *Poems by Emily Dickinson*, Second Series, published November 9.

1894 *Letters of Emily Dickinson* published, November 21.

1895 Death of Austin Dickinson, August 16.

1896 *Poems of Emily Dickinson*, Third Series, published September 1.

1899 Death of Lavinia Dickinson, August 23.

1913 Death of Susan Gilbert Dickinson, May 12.

1914 Publication of *The Single Hound,* edited by Martha Dickinson Bianchi.

1924 *The Life and Letters of Emily Dickinson,* edited by Martha Dickinson Bianchi.

1929 *Further Poems of Emily Dickinson,* edited by Martha Dickinson Bianchi.

1935 *Unpublished Poems of Emily Dickinson,* edited by Martha Dickinson Bianchi.

1937 *The Poems of Emily Dickinson,* a collected edition, edited by Martha Dickinson Bianchi and Alfred Leete Hampson.

1943 Death of Martha Dickinson Bianchi, December 21.

1945 *Bolts of Melody: New Poems of Emily Dickinson,* edited by Mabel Loomis Todd and Millicent Todd Bingham.

1950 Alfred Leete Hampson, heir of Martha Dickinson Bianchi, sold the manuscripts of Emily Dickinson to Gilbert H. Montague who presented them to the Harvard College Library.

1955 *The Poems of Emily Dickinson,* in three volumes, edited by Thomas H. Johnson.

1958 *The Letters of Emily Dickinson,* in three volumes, edited by Thomas H. Johnson.

1

Success is counted sweetest *
By those who ne'er succeed.
To comprehend a nectar
Requires sorest need.

Not one of all the purple host
Who took the flag to-day
Can tell the definition,
So clear, of victory,

As he, defeated, dying,
On whose forbidden ear
The distant strains of triumph
Break, agonized and clear.

* Notes to poems appear together beginning on page
153.

2

Arcturus is his other name,—
I'd rather call him star!
It's so unkind of science
To go and interfere!

I pull a flower from the woods,—
A monster with a glass
Computes the stamens in a breath,
And has her in a class.

Whereas I took the butterfly
Aforetime in my hat,
He sits erect in cabinets,
The clover-bells forgot.

What once was heaven, is zenith now.
Where I proposed to go
When time's brief masquerade was done,
Is mapped, and charted too!

What if the poles should frisk about
And stand upon their heads!
I hope I'm ready for the worst,
Whatever prank betides!

Perhaps the kingdom of Heaven's changed!
I hope the children there
Won't be new-fashioned when I come,
And laugh at me, and stare!

I hope the father in the skies
Will lift his little girl,—
Old-fashioned, naughty, everything,—
Over the stile of pearl!

3

As by the dead we love to sit,
Become so wondrous dear,
As for the lost we grapple,
Though all the rest are here,—

In broken mathematics
We estimate our prize,
Vast, in its fading ratio,
To our penurious eyes!

4

One dignity delays for all,
One mitred afternoon.
None can avoid this purple,
None evade this crown.

Coach it insures, and footmen,
Chamber and state and throng;
Bells, also, in the village,
As we ride grand along.

What dignified attendants,
What service when we pause!
How loyally at parting
Their hundred hats they raise!

How pomp surpassing ermine,
When simple you and I
Present our meek escutcheon,
And claim the rank to die!

5

To fight aloud is very brave,
But gallanter, I know,
Who charge within the bosom,
The cavalry of woe.

Who win, and nations do not see,
Who fall, and none observe,
Whose dying eyes no country
Regards with patriot love.

We trust, in plumed procession,
For such the angels go,
Rank after rank, with even feet
And uniforms of snow.

ne back,

when skies put on
The old, old sophistries of June,—
A blue and gold mistake.

Oh, fraud that cannot cheat the bee,
Almost thy plausibility
Induces my belief,

Till ranks of seeds their witness bear,
And softly through the altered air
Hurries a timid leaf!

Oh, sacrament of summer days,
Oh, last communion in the haze,
Permit a child to join,

Thy sacred emblems to partake,
Thy consecrated bread to break,
Taste thine immortal wine!

7

Flowers—well, if anybody
Can the ecstasy define,
Half a transport, half a trouble,
With which flowers humble men,
Anybody find the fountain
From which floods so contra flow,
I will give him all the daisies
Which upon the hillside blow.

Too much pathos in their faces
For a simple breast like mine.
Butterflies from San Domingo
Cruising round the purple line
Have a system of aesthetics
Far superior to mine.

8

An altered look about the hills;
A Tyrian light the village fills;
A wider sunrise in the dawn;
A deeper twilight on the lawn;
A print of a vermilion foot;
A purple finger on the slope;
A flippant fly upon the pane;
A spider at his trade again;
An added strut in chanticleer;
A flower expected everywhere;
An axe shrill singing in the woods;
Fern-odors on untravelled roads,—
All this, and more I cannot tell,
A furtive look you know as well,
And Nicodemus' mystery *
Receives its annual reply.

9

I taste a liquor never brewed,
From tankards scooped in pearl;
Not all the vats upon the Rhine
Yield such an alcohol!

Inebriate of air am I,
And debauchee of dew,
Reeling, through endless summer days,
From inns of molten blue.

When landlords turn the drunken bee
Out of the foxglove's door,
When butterflies renounce their drams,
I shall but drink the more!

Till seraphs swing their snowy hats,
And saints to windows run,
To see the little tippler
Leaning against the sun!

10

Safe in their alabaster chambers,
Untouched by morning and untouched by noon,
Sleep the meek members of the resurrection,
Rafter of satin, and roof of stone.

Light laughs the breeze in her castle of sunshine;
Babbles the bee in a stolid ear;
Pipe the sweet birds in ignorant cadence,—
Ah, what sagacity perished here!

Grand go the years in the crescent above them;
Worlds scoop their arcs, and firmaments row,
Diadems drop and Doges surrender,
Soundless as dots on a disc of snow.

11

Hope is the thing with feathers
That perches in the soul,
And sings the tune without the words,
And never stops at all,

And sweetest in the gale is heard;
And sore must be the storm
That could abash the little bird
That kept so many warm.

I've heard it in the chillest land,
And on the strangest sea;
Yet, never, in extremity,
It asked a crumb of me.

12

There's a certain slant of light,
On winter afternoons,
That oppresses, like the weight
Of cathedral tunes.

Heavenly hurt it gives us;
We can find no scar,
But internal difference
Where the meanings are.

None may teach it anything,
'Tis the seal, despair,—
An imperial affliction
Sent us of the air.

When it comes, the landscape listens,
Shadows hold their breath;
When it goes, 'tis like the distance
On the look of death.

13

I felt a funeral in my brain,
   And mourners, to and fro,
Kept treading, treading, till it seemed
   That sense was breaking through.

And when they all were seated,
   A service like a drum
Kept beating, beating, till I thought
   My mind was going numb.

And then I heard them lift a box,
   And creak across my soul
With those same boots of lead, again.
   Then space began to toll

As all the heavens were a bell,
   And Being but an ear,
And I and silence some strange race,
   Wrecked, solitary, here.

14

'Tis so appalling it exhilarates!
So over-horror it half captivates!
The Soul stares after it, secure,
To know the worst leaves no dread more.

To scan a ghost is faint,
But grappling conquers it.
How easy, torment, now—
Suspense kept sawing so.

The truth is bald and cold,
But that will hold.
If any are not sure,
We show them prayer—
But we who know
Stop hoping now.

Looking at Death is dying—
Just let go the breath,
And not the pillow at your cheek
So slumbereth.

Others can wrestle, yours is done,
And so of woe bleak dreaded, come—
It sets the fright at liberty,
And terror's free—
Gay, ghastly holiday!

15

Of bronze and blaze
The north, to-night!
So adequate its forms,
So preconcerted with itself,
So distant to alarms,—
An unconcern so sovereign
To universe, or me,

It paints my simple spirit
With tints of majesty,
Till I take vaster attitudes,
And strut upon my stem,
Disdaining men and oxygen,
For arrogance of them.

My splendors are menagerie;
But their competeless show
Will entertain the centuries
When I am, long ago,
An island in dishonored grass,
Whom none but daisies know.

16

I reason, earth is short,
And anguish absolute,
And many hurt;
But what of that?

I reason, we could die:
The best vitality
Cannot excel decay;
But what of that?

I reason that in heaven
Somehow, it will be even,
Some new equation given;
But what of that?

17

The soul selects her own society,
Then shuts the door;
On her divine majority
Obtrude no more.

Unmoved, she notes the chariot's pausing
At her low gate;
Unmoved, an emperor is kneeling
Upon her mat.

I've known her from an ample nation
Choose one;
Then close the valves of her attention
Like stone.

18

Of all the sounds despatched abroad,
There's not a charge to me
Like that old measure in the boughs,
That phraseless melody.

The wind does, working like a hand
Whose fingers comb the sky,
Then quiver down, with tufts of tune
Permitted gods and me.

Inheritance it is to us
Beyond the art to earn,
Beyond the trait to take away
By robber, since the gain

Is gotten not of fingers,
And inner than the bone,
Hid golden for the whole of days,
And even in the urn

I cannot vouch the merry dust
Do not arise and play
In some odd pattern of its own
Some quainter holiday.

When winds go round and round in bands,
And thrum upon the door,
And birds take places overhead,
To bear them orchestra,

I crave him grace of summer boughs,
If such an outcast be,
Who never heard that fleshless chant
Rise solemn on the tree,

As if some caravan of sound
Off deserts, in the sky,

Had parted rank,
Then knit, and swept
In seamless company.

19

There came a day at summer's full
Entirely for me;
I thought that such were for the saints,
Where revelations be.

The sun, as common, went abroad,
The flowers, accustomed, blew,
As if no sail the solstice passed
That maketh all things new.

The time was scarce profaned by speech;
The symbol of a word
Was needless, as at sacrament
The wardrobe of our Lord.

Each was to each the sealéd church,
Permitted to commune this time,
Lest we too awkward show
At supper of the Lamb.

The hours slid fast, as hours will,
Clutched tight by greedy hands;
So faces on two decks look back,
Bound to opposing lands.

And so, when all the time had failed,
Without external sound,
Each bound the other's crucifix,
We gave no other bond.

Sufficient troth that we shall rise—
Deposed, at length, the grave—
To that new marriage, justified
Through Calvaries of Love!

Before I got my eye put out,
I liked as well to see
As other creatures that have eyes,
And know no other way.

But were it told to me, to-day,
That I might have the sky
For mine, I tell you that my heart
Would split, for size of me.

The meadows mine, the mountains mine,—
All forests, stintless stars,
As much of noon as I could take
Between my finite eyes.

The motions of the dipping birds,
The lightning's jointed road,
For mine to look at when I liked,—
The news would strike me dead!

So, safer, guess, with just my soul
Upon the window-pane
Where other creatures put their eyes,
Incautious of the sun.

21

A bird came down the walk:
He did not know I saw;
He bit an angle-worm in halves
And ate the fellow, raw.

And then he drank a dew
From a convenient grass,
And then hopped sidewise to the wall
To let a beetle pass.

He glanced with rapid eyes
That hurried all abroad,—
They looked like frightened beads, I thought
He stirred his velvet head

Like one in danger; cautious,
I offered him a crumb,
And he unrolled his feathers
And rowed him softer home

Than oars divide the ocean,
Too silver for a seam,
Or butterflies, off banks of noon,
Leap, plashless, as they swim.

22

It struck me every day;
   The lightning was as new
As if the cloud that instant slit
   And let the fire through.

It burned me in the night,
   It blistered to my dream,
It sickened fresh upon my sight
   With every morn that came.

I thought that storm was brief—
   The maddest, quickest by;
But Nature lost the date of this
   And left it in the sky.

23

Dare you see a soul at the white heat?
　　Then crouch within the door.
Red is the fire's common tint;
　　But when the vivid ore

Has sated flame's conditions,
　　Its quivering substance plays
Without a color but the light
　　Of unanointed blaze.

Least village boasts its blacksmith,
　　Whose anvil's even din
Stands symbol for the finer forge
　　That soundless tugs within,

Refining these impatient ores
　　With hammer and with blaze,
Until the designated light
　　Repudiate the forge.

24

The angle of a landscape
That every time I wake
Between my curtain and the wall
Upon an ample crack

Like a Venetian, waiting,
Accosts my open eye,
Is just a bough of apples
Held slanting in the sky,

The pattern of a chimney,
The forehead of a hill,
Sometimes a vane's forefinger—
But that's occasional.

The seasons shift my picture.
Upon my emerald bough
I wake to find no emeralds;
Then diamonds which the snow

From polar caskets fetched me.
The chimney and the hill
And just the steeple's finger,
These never stir at all.

25

There is a flower that bees prefer,
And butterflies desire;
To gain the purple democrat
The humming-birds aspire.

And whatsoever insect pass,
A honey bears away
Proportioned to his several dearth
And her capacity.

Her face is rounder than the moon,
And ruddier than the gown
Of orchis in the pasture,
Or rhododendron worn.

She doth not wait for June;
Before the world is green
Her sturdy little countenance
Against the wind is seen,

Contending with the grass,
Near kinsman to herself,
For privilege of sod and sun,
Sweet litigants for life.

And when the hills are full,
And newer fashions blow,
Doth not retract a single spice
For pang of jealousy.

Her public is the noon,
Her providence the sun,
Her progress by the bee proclaimed
In sovereign, swerveless tune.

The bravest of the host,
Surrendering the last,

Nor even of defeat aware
When cancelled by the frost.

26

No rack can torture me,
My soul's at liberty,
Behind this mortal bone
There knits a bolder one

You cannot prick with saw
Nor rend with scimitar.
Two bodies therefore be;
Bind one, and one will flee.

The eagle of his nest
No easier divest
And gain the sky,
Than mayest thou,

Except thyself may be
Thine enemy;
Captivity is consciousness,
So's liberty.

What soft, cherubic creatures
    These gentlewomen are!
One would as soon assault a plush
    Or violate a star.

Such dimity convictions,
    A horror so refined
Of freckled human nature,
    Of Deity ashamed,—

It's such a common glory,
    A fisherman's degree!
Redemption, brittle lady,
    Be so ashamed of thee.

28

I read my sentence steadily,
Reviewed it with my eyes,
To see that I made no mistake
In its extremest clause,—

The date, and manner of the shame;
And then the pious form
That "God have mercy" on the soul
The jury voted him.

I made my soul familiar
With her extremity,
That at the last it should not be
A novel agony,

But she and Death, acquainted,
Meet tranquilly as friends,
Salute and pass without a hint—
And there the matter ends.

29

A charm invests a face
Imperfectly beheld,—
The lady dare not lift her veil
For fear it be dispelled.

But peers beyond her mesh,
And wishes, and denies,—
Lest interview annul a want
That image satisfies.

30

Much madness is divinest sense
To a discerning eye;
Much sense the starkest madness.
'Tis the majority
In this, as all, prevails.
Assent, and you are sane;
Demur,—you're straightway dangerous,
And handled with a chain.

31

This is my letter to the world,
    That never wrote to me,—
The simple news that Nature told,
    With tender majesty.

Her message is committed
    To hands I cannot see;
For love of her, sweet countrymen,
    Judge tenderly of me!

I died for beauty, but was scarce
Adjusted in the tomb,
When one who died for truth was lain
In an adjoining room.

He questioned softly why I failed?
"For beauty," I replied.
"And I for truth,—the two are one;
We brethren are," he said.

And so, as kinsmen met a night,
We talked between the rooms,
Until the moss had reached our lips,
And covered up our names.

The outer from the inner
Derives its magnitude—
'Tis duke, or dwarf, according
As is the central mood—

The fine unvarying axis
That regulates the wheel,
Though spokes spin more conspicuous
And fling a dust the while.

The inner paints the outer;
The brush without the hand
Its picture publishes, precise
As is the inner brand

On fine arterial canvas—
A check, perchance a brow.
The stars' whole secret in the lake
Eyes were not meant to know.

34

Like eyes that looked on wastes,
Incredulous of ought *
But blank and steady wilderness
Diversified by night—

Just infinites of nought
As far as it could see,
So looked the face I looked upon.
So looked itself on me.

I offered it no help
Because the cause was mine,
The misery a compact
As hopeless as divine.

Neither would be absolved,
Neither would be a queen
Without the other—therefore
We perish, though we reign.

35

I live with him, I see his face;
    I go no more away
For visitor, or sundown;
    Death's single privacy,

The only one forestalling mine,
    And that by right that he
Presents a claim invisible,
    No wedlock granted me.

I live with him, I hear his voice,
    I stand alive to-day
To witness to the certainty
    Of immortality

Taught me by Time,—the lower way,
    Conviction every day,—
That life like this is endless,
    Be judgment what it may.

36

I heard a fly buzz when I died;
   The stillness round my form
Was like the stillness in the air
   Between the heaves of storm.

The eyes beside had wrung them dry,
   And breaths were gathering sure
For that last onset, when the king
   Be witnessed in his power.

I willed my keepsakes, signed away
   What portion of me I
Could make assignable,—and then
   There interposed a fly,

With blue, uncertain, stumbling buzz,
   Between the light and me;
And then the windows failed, and then
   I could not see to see.

37

A night there lay the days between,
The day that was before
And day that was behind were one,
And now 'twas night was here—

Slow night, that must be watched away
As grains upon a shore,
Too imperceptible to note
Till it be night no more.

38

We cover thee, sweet face.
　　Not that we tire of thee,
But that thyself fatigue of us;
　　Remember, as thou flee,
We follow thee until
　　Thou notice us no more,
And then, reluctant, turn away
　　To con thee o'er and o'er,
And blame the scanty love
　　We were content to show,
Augmented, sweet, a hundred fold
　　If thou would'st take it now.

39

Better than music, for I who heard it,
I was used to the birds before;
This was different, 'twas translation
Of all tunes I knew, and more;

'Twasn't contained like other stanza,
No one could play it the second time
But the composer, perfect Mozart,
Perish with him that keyless rhyme!

So children, assured that brooks in Eden
Bubbled a better melody,
Quaintly infer Eve's great surrender,
Urging the feet that would not fly.

Children matured are wiser, mostly,
Eden a legend dimly told,
Eve and the anguish grandame's story—
But I was telling a tune I heard.

Not such a strain the church baptizes
When the last saint goes up the aisles,
Not such a stanza shakes the silence
When the redemption strikes her bells.

Let me not lose its smallest cadence,
Humming for promise when alone,
Humming until my faint rehearsal
Drop into tune around the throne!

40

It was not death, for I stood up,
And all the dead lie down;
It was not night, for all the bells
Put out their tongues, for noon.

It was not frost, for on my flesh
I felt siroccos crawl,—
Nor fire, for just my marble feet
Could keep a chancel cool.

And yet it tasted like them all;
The figures I have seen
Set orderly, for burial,
Reminded me of mine,

As if my life were shaven
And fitted to a frame,
And could not breathe without a key;
And 'twas like midnight, some,

When everything that ticked has stopped,
And space stares, all around,
Or grisly frosts, first autumn morns,
Repeal the beating ground.

But most like chaos,—stopless, cool,—
Without a chance or spar,
Or even a report of land
To justify despair.

41

The soul has bandaged moments
When too appalled to stir;
She feels some ghastly fright come up
And stop to look at her,
Salute her with long fingers,
Caress her freezing hair,
Sip, goblin, from the very lips
The lover hovered o'er—
Unworthy that a thought so mean
Accost a theme so fair.

The soul has moments of escape
When, bursting all the doors,
She dances like a bomb abroad,
And swings upon the hours
As do the bee, delirious borne,
Long dungeoned from his rose,
Touch liberty—then know no more
But noon and paradise.

The soul's retaken moments
When, felon, led along
With shackles on the plumèd feet
And rivets in the song,
The horror welcomes her again—
These are not brayed of tongue.

42

Departed to the judgment,
A mighty afternoon;
Great clouds like ushers leaning,
Creation looking on.

The flesh surrendered, cancelled,
The bodiless begun;
Two worlds, like audiences, disperse
And leave the soul alone.

43

To hear an oriole sing
May be a common thing,
Or only a divine.

It is not of the bird
Who sings the same, unheard,
As unto crowd.

The fashion of the ear
Attireth that it hear
In dun or fair.

So whether it be rune,
Or whether it be none,
Is of within;

The "tune is in the tree,"
The sceptic showeth me;
"No, sir! In thee!"

Mine by the right of the white election!
Mine by the royal seal!
Mine by the sign in the scarlet prison
Bars cannot conceal!

Mine, here in vision and in veto!
Mine, by the grave's repeal
Titled, confirmed,—delirious charter!
Mine, while the ages steal!

45

I tried to think a lonelier thing
Than any I had seen—
Some polar expiation,
An omen in the bone

Of death's tremendous nearness—
I probed retrieveless things
My duplicate to borrow.
A haggard comfort springs

From the belief that somewhere
Within the clutch of thought
There dwells one other creature
Of Heavenly love forgot.

I plucked at our partition,
As one should pry the walls
Between himself and horror's twin
Within opposing cells.

I almost strove to clasp his hand,
Such luxury it grew
That as myself could pity him
Perhaps he pitied me.

46

The heart asks pleasure first,
And then, excuse from pain;
And then, those little anodynes
That deaden suffering;

And then, to go to sleep;
And then, if it should be
The will of its Inquisitor,
The liberty to die.

47

I've seen a dying eye
Run round and round a room
In search of something, as it seemed,
Then cloudier become;

And then, obscure with fog,
And then be soldered down,
Without disclosing what it be,
'Twere blessed to have seen.

I measure every grief I meet *
   With analytic eyes;
I wonder if it weighs like mine,
   Or has an easier size.

I wonder if they bore it long,
   Or did it just begin—
I could not tell the date of mine,
   It feels so old a pain.

I wonder if it hurts to live,
   And if they have to try,
And whether—could they choose between—
   It would not be to die.

I note that some—gone patient long—
   At length renew their smile:
An imitation of a light
   That has so little oil.

I wonder if when years have piled,
   Some thousands, on the harm
That hurt them early, such a lapse
   Could give them any balm.

Or would they go on aching still
   Through centuries of nerve,
Enlightened to a larger pain
   In contrast with the love.

The grieved are many, I am told;
   There is the various cause;
Death is but one and comes but once
   And only nails the eyes.

There's grief of want, and grief of cold—
   A sort they call "despair";

There's banishment from native eyes
    In sight of native air.

And though I may not guess the kind
    Correctly, yet to me
A piercing comfort it affords
    In passing Calvary,

To note the fashions of the cross,
    And how they're mostly worn,
Still fascinated to presume
    That some are like my own.

49

We learned the whole of love,
The alphabet, the words,
A chapter, then the mighty book—
Then revelation closed.

But in each other's eyes
An ignorance beheld
Diviner than the childhood's,
And each to each a child

Attempted to expound
What neither understood.
Alas, that wisdom is so large
And truth so manifold!

50

I like to see it lap the miles,
And lick the valleys up,
And stop to feed itself at tanks;
And then, prodigious, step

Around a pile of mountains,
And, supercilious, peer
In shanties by the sides of roads;
And then a quarry pare

To fit its sides, and crawl between,
Complaining all the while
In horrid, hooting stanza;
Then chase itself down hill

And neigh like Boanerges;
Then, punctual as a star,
Stop—docile and omnipotent—
At its own stable door.

51

The spider holds a silver ball
In unperceivéd hands
And dancing softly to himself
His yarn of pearl unwinds.

He plies from naught to naught
In unsubstantial trade,
Supplants our tapestries with his
In half the period—

An hour to rear supreme
His theories of light,
Then dangle from the housewife's broom,
His sophistries forgot.

52

Our journey had advanced;
Our feet were almost come
To that odd fork in Being's road,
Eternity by term.

Our pace took sudden awe,
Our feet reluctant led.
Before were cities, but between,
The forest of the dead.

Retreat was out of hope,—
Behind, a sealéd route,
Eternity's white flag before,
And God at every gate.

53

'Twas a long parting, but the time
For interview had come;
Before the judgment-seat of God,
The last and second time

These fleshless lovers met,
A heaven in a gaze,
A heaven of heavens, the privilege
Of one another's eyes.

No lifetime set on them,
Apparelled as the new
Unborn, except they had beheld,
Born everlasting now.

Was bridal e'er like this?
A paradise, the host,
And cherubim and seraphim
The most familiar guest.

54

I watched the moon around the house
Until upon a pane
She stopped—a traveller's privilege—
For rest, and thereupon

I gazed, as at a stranger
The lady in the town
Doth think no incivility
To lift her glass upon.

But never stranger justified
The curiosity
Like mine, for not a foot nor hand
Nor formula had she,

But like a head a guillotine
Slid carelessly away,
Revolved independent, amber,
Sustain her in the sky;

Or like a stemless flower
Upheld in rolling air
By finer gravitations
Than bind philosopher.

No hunger had she, nor an inn
Her toilette to suffice,
Nor avocation, nor concern
For little mysteries

As harass us—like life and death
And afterward, or nay—
But seemed engrossed to absolute
With shining and the sky.

The privilege to scrutinize
Was scarce upon my eyes,

When with a silver practice
She vaulted out of gaze.

And next I met her on a cloud,
Myself too far below
To follow her superior road
Or its advantage blue.

55

The lightning playeth all the while,
But when he singeth, then
Ourselves are conscious he exist,
And we approach him stern,

With insulators and a glove,
Whose short sepulchral bass
Alarms us, though his yellow feet
May pass and counterpass

Upon the ropes above our head
Continual, with the news,
Nor we so much as check our speech
Nor stop to cross ourselves.

56

Pain has an element of blank;
It cannot recollect
When it began, or if there were
A day when it was not.

It has no future but itself,
Its infinite realms contain
Its past, enlightened to perceive
New periods of pain.

57

Of all the souls that stand create
I have elected one.
When sense from spirit files away
And subterfuge is done;

When that which is and that which was
Apart, intrinsic, stand,
And this brief tragedy of flesh
Is sifted like a sand;

When figures show their royal front
And mists are carved away,—
Behold the atom I preferred
To all the lists of clay!

58

On the bleakness of my lot
  Bloom I strove to raise.
Late, my acre of a rock
  Yielded grape and maize.

Soil of flint if steadfast tilled
  Will reward the hand;
Seed of palm by Libyan sun
  Fructified in sand.

59

Because I could not stop for Death,
He kindly stopped for me;
The carriage held but just ourselves
And Immortality.

We slowly drove, he knew no haste,
And I had put away
My labor, and my leisure too,
For his civility.

We passed the school where children played
At wrestling in a ring;
We passed the fields of gazing grain,
We passed the setting sun.

We paused before a house that seemed
A swelling of the ground;
The roof was scarcely visible,
The cornice but a mound.

Since then 'tis centuries; but each
Feels shorter than the day
I first surmised the horses' heads
Were toward eternity.

Remorse is memory awake,
Her companies astir,—
A presence of departed acts
At window and at door.

Its past set down before the soul,
And lighted with a match,
Perusal to facilitate
Of its condensed despatch.

Remorse is cureless,—the disease
Not even God can heal;
For 'tis His institution,—
The complement of hell.

61

One blessing had I than the rest
    So larger to my eyes
That I stopped gauging, satisfied,
    For this enchanted size.

It was the limit of my dream,
    The focus of my prayer—
A perfect, paralyzing bliss
    Contented as despair.

I knew no more of want or cold,
    Phantasms both become,
For this new value in the soul,
    Supremest earthly sum.

The heaven below the heaven above
    Obscured with ruddier blue,
Life's latitudes leant over-full;
    The judgment perished, too.

Why bliss so scantily disburse,
    Why Paradise defer,
Why floods be served to us in bowls—
    I speculate no more.

62

The hallowing of pain,
Like hallowing of heaven,
Obtains at corporeal cost.
The summit is not given

To him who strives severe
At bottom of the hill,
But he who has achieved the top—
All is the price of all.

63

The birds begun at four o'clock—*
Their period for dawn—
A music numerous as space
And measureless as noon.

I could not count their force,
Their voices did expend
As brook by brook bestows itself
To magnify the pond.

Their witnesses were not,
Except occasional man
In homely industry arrayed
To overtake the morn.

Nor was it for applause
That I could ascertain,
But independent ecstasy
Of Deity and Men.

By six the flood had done,
No tumult there had been
Of dressing or departure,
Yet all the band was gone.

The sun engrossed the east,
The day controlled the world,
The miracle that introduced
Forgotten as fulfilled.

Bereaved of all, I went abroad,
　No less bereaved to be
Upon a new peninsula,—
　The grave preceded me,

Obtained my lodgings ere myself,
　And when I sought my bed,
The grave it was, reposed upon
　The pillow for my head.

I waked, to find it first awake,
　I rose,—it followed me;
I tried to drop it in the crowd,
　To lose it in the sea,

In cups of artificial drowse
　To sleep its shape away,—
The grave was finished, but the spade
　Remained in memory.

65

Through the straight pass of suffering
The martyrs even trod,
Their feet upon temptation,
Their faces upon God.

A stately, shriven company;
Convulsion playing round,
Harmless as streaks of meteor
Upon a planet's bound.

Their faith the everlasting troth;
Their expectation fair;
The needle to the north degree
Wades so, through polar air.

66

A light exists in spring
   Not present on the year
At any other period.
   When March is scarcely here

A color stands abroad
   On solitary hills
That science cannot overtake,
   But human nature feels.

It waits upon the lawn;
   It shows the furthest tree
Upon the furthest slope we know;
   It almost speaks to me.

Then, as horizons step,
   Or noons report away,
Without the formula of sound,
   It passes, and we stay;

A quality of loss
   Afflicting our content,
As trade had suddenly encroached
   Upon a sacrament.

67

The robin is the one
That interrupts the morn
With hurried, few, express reports
When March is scarcely on.

The robin is the one
That overflows the noon
With her cherubic quantity,
An April but begun.

The robin is the one
That speechless from her nest
Submits that home and certainty
And sanctity are best.

68

Ample make this bed.
Make this bed with awe;
In it wait till judgment break
Excellent and fair.

Be its mattress straight,
Be its pillow round;
Let no sunrise' yellow noise
Interrupt this ground.

69

Dying! To be afraid of thee
One must to thine artillery
   Have left exposed a friend.
Than thine old arrow is a shot
Delivered straighter to the heart,
   The leaving love behind.

Not for itself the dust is shy,
But, enemy, belovéd be
   Thy batteries' divorce.
Fight sternly in a dying eye
Two armies, love and certainty,
   And love and the reverse.

70

There is a finished feeling
Experienced at graves—
A leisure of the future,
A wilderness of size,

By death's bold exhibition
Preciser what we are
And the eternal function
Enabled to infer.

71

This chasm, sweet, upon my life,
I mention it to you;
When sunrise through a fissure drop
The day must follow too.

If we demur, its gaping sides
Disclose as 'twere a tomb
Ourself am lying straight wherein,
The favorite of doom.

When it has just contained a life
Then, darling, it will close,
And yet, so bolder every day,
So turbulent it grows,

I'm tempted half to stitch it up
With a remaining breath
I should not miss in yielding, though
To him it would be death.

And so I bear it big about
My burial before—
A life quite ready to depart
Can harass me no more.

72

Split the lark and you'll find the music,
    Bulb after bulb, in silver rolled,
Scantily dealt to the summer morning,
    Saved for your ear when lutes be old.

Loose the flood, you shall find it patent,
    Gush after gush, reserved for you;
Scarlet experiment! sceptic Thomas,
    Now, do you doubt that your bird was true?

73

Light is sufficient to itself.
If others want to see,
It can be had on window panes
Some hours of the day,

But not for compensation—
It holds as large a glow
To squirrel in the Hammaleh
Precisely, as to you.

Those who have been in the grave the longest,
Those who begin today,

practice.

d least attempt it,
exploit
lieve annuls the power
ommunicate.

74

To my quick ear the leaves conferred;
    The bushes they were bells;
I could not find a privacy
    From Nature's sentinels

In cave if I presumed to hide,
    The walls began to tell;
Creation seemed a mighty crack
    To make me visible.

75

A cloud withdrew from the sky.
Superior glory be,
But that cloud and its auxiliaries
Are forever lost to me.

Had I but further scanned,
Had I secured the glow
In an hermetic memory
It had availed me now.

Never to pass the angel
With a glance and a bow
Till I am firm in Heaven
Is my intention now.

Equally p...
Death is t...

Foot of th...
It is the w...
Once to a...
Once to c...

To my quick ear the leaves conferred;
    The bushes they were bells;
I could not find a privacy
    From Nature's sentinels.

In cave if I presumed to hide,
    The walls began to tell;
Creation seemed a mighty crack
    To make me visible.

A cloud withdrew from the sky.
Superior glory be,
But that cloud and its auxiliaries
Are forever lost to me.

Had I but further scanned,
Had I secured the glow
In an hermetic memory
It had availed me now.

Never to pass the angel
With a glance and a bow
Till I am firm in Heaven
Is my intention now.

Those who have been in the grave the longest,
Those who begin today,
Equally...from our practice.
Death is the further way.

Foot of the bold did least attempt it,
It is the white... exploit
Once to achieve annuls the power
Once to communicate.

A coffin is a small domain
Yet able to contain
A rudiment of paradise
In its diminished plane.

A grave is a restricted breadth
Yet ampler than the sun
And all the seas he populates
And lands he looks upon,

To him who on its low repose
Bestows a single friend—
Circumference without relief,
Or estimate, or end.

81

A loss of something ever felt I.
The first that I could recollect
Bereft I was, of what I knew not,
Too young that any should suspect

A mourner lurked among the children.
I notwithstanding stole about
As one bemoaning a dominion,
Itself the only prince cast out.

Elder today, a session wiser—
And fainter too, as wiseness is—
I find myself still softly searching
For my delinquent palaces,

And a suspicion like a finger
Touches my forehead now and then,
That I am looking oppositely
For the site of the kingdom of heaven.

82

Death is a dialogue between
The spirit and the dust.
"Dissolve," says Death. The Spirit, "Sir,
I have another trust."

Death doubts it, argues from the ground.
The spirit turns away,
Just laying off, for evidence,
An overcoat of clay.

83

This merit hath the worst,—
It cannot be again.
When Fate hath taunted last
And thrown her furthest stone,

The maimed may pause and breathe,
And glance securely round.
The deer invites no longer
Than it eludes the hound.

84

A narrow fellow in the grass
Occasionally rides;
You may have met him,—did you not?
His notice sudden is.

The grass divides as with a comb,
A spotted shaft is seen;
And then it closes at your feet
And opens further on.

He likes a boggy acre,
A floor too cool for corn.
Yet when a child, and barefoot,
I more than once, at morn,

Have passed, I thought, a whip-lash
Unbraiding in the sun,—
When, stooping to secure it,
It wrinkled, and was gone.

Several of nature's people
I know, and they know me;
I feel for them a transport
Of cordiality;

But never met this fellow,
Attended or alone,
Without a tighter breathing,
And zero at the bone.

85

Partake as doth the bee,
   Abstemiously;
A rose is an estate
   In Sicily.

86

Crumbling is not an instant's act,
A fundamental pause;
Dilapidation's processes
Are organized decays.

'Tis first a cobweb on the soul,
A cuticle of dust,
A borer in the axis,
An elemental rust.

Ruin is formal, devil's work,
Consecutive and slow—
Fail in an instant no man did,
Slipping is crash's law.

87

There is no silence in the earth so silent
  As that endured
Which, uttered, would discourage nature
  And haunt the world.

88

The products of my farm are these,
Sufficient for my own
And here and there a benefit
Unto a neighbor's bin.

With us 'tis harvest all the year,
For when the frosts begin,
We just reverse the zodiac
And fetch the acres in.

89

I never saw a moor,
I never saw the sea;
Yet know I how the heather looks,
And what a wave must be.

I never spoke with God,
Nor visited in heaven;
Yet certain am I of the spot
As if the chart were given.

90

Not to discover weakness is
The mystery of strength;
Impregnability inheres
As much through consciousness

Of faith of others in itself,
As elemental nerve.
Behind the most consummate clock
What skillful pointers move!

91

There is a zone whose even years
No solstice interrupt,
Whose sun constructs perpetual noon,
Whose perfect seasons wait;

Whose summer set in summer till
The centuries of June
And centuries of August fuse
And consciousness is noon.

92

Let down the bars, O Death!
The tired flocks come in
Whose bleating ceases to repeat,
Whose wandering is done.

Thine is the stillest night,
Thine the securest fold;
Too near thou art for seeking thee,
Too tender to be told.

Farther in summer than the birds,
Pathetic from the grass,
A minor nation celebrates
Its unobtrusive mass.

No ordinance is seen,
So gradual the grace,
A pensive custom it becomes,
Enlarging loneliness.

Antiquest felt at noon
When August, burning low,
Calls forth this spectral canticle,
Repose to gratify.

Remit as yet no grace,
No furrow on the glow,
Yet a druidic difference
Enhances nature now.

Title divine is mine
The Wife without
The Sign.
Acute degree
Conferred on me—
Empress of Calvary.
Royal all but the
Crown—
Betrothed, without the swoon
God gives us women
When two hold
Garnet to garnet,
Gold to gold—
Born—Bridalled—
Shrouded—
In a day
Tri-Victory—
   "My Husband"
Women say
Stroking the melody,
Is this the way?

95

Superiority to fate
    Is difficult to learn.
'Tis not conferred by any,
    But possible to earn

A pittance at a time,
    Until, to her surprise,
The soul with strict economy
    Subsists till Paradise.

96

At half-past three a single bird
Unto a silent sky
Propounded but a single term
Of cautious melody.

At half-past four, experiment
Had subjugated test,
And lo! her silver principle
Supplanted all the rest.

At half-past seven, element
Nor implement was seen,
And place was where the presence was,
Circumference between.

97

Ended, ere it begun—
The title was scarcely told
When the preface perished from consciousness,
The story, unrevealed.

Had it been mine, to print!
Had it been yours, to read!
That it was not our privilege
The interdict of God.

98

My cocoon tightens, colors tease,
I'm feeling for the air;
A dim capacity for wings
Degrades the dress I wear.

A power of butterfly must be
The aptitude to fly,
Meadows of majesty concedes
And easy sweeps of sky.

So I must baffle at the hint
And cipher at the sign,
And make much blunder, if at last
I take the clew divine.

99

The last night that she lived,
It was a common night,
Except the dying; this to us
Made nature different.

We noticed smallest things,—
Things overlooked before,
By this great light upon our minds
Italicized, as 'twere.

That others could exist
While she must finish quite,
A jealousy for her arose
So nearly infinite.

We waited while she passed;
It was a narrow time,
Too jostled were our souls to speak,
At length the notice came.

She mentioned, and forgot;
Then lightly as a reed
Bent to the water, shivered scarce,
Consented, and was dead.

And we, we placed the hair,
And drew the head erect;
And then an awful leisure was,
Our faith to regulate.

100

The murmuring of bees has ceased;
    But murmuring of some
Posterior, prophetic,
    Has simultaneous come,—
The lower metres of the year,
    When nature's laugh is done,—
The Revelations of the book
    Whose Genesis is June.

101

A great hope fell, you heard no noise,
The ruin was within.
Oh, cunning wreck that told no tale
And let no witness in!

The mind was built for mighty freight,
For dread occasion planned,
How often foundering at sea,
Ostensibly on land!

A not admitting of the wound
Until it grew so wide
That all my life had entered it
And there was room beside.

A closing of the simple lid
That opened to the sun
Until the sovereign Carpenter
Perpetual nail it down.

102

"Shall I take thee?" the poet said
To the propounded word.
"Be stationed with the candidates
Till I have further tried."

The poet probed philology
And when about to ring
For the suspended candidate,
There came unsummoned in

That portion of the vision
The word applied to fill.
Not unto nomination
The cherubim reveal.

103

Tell all the truth but tell it slant,
Success in circuit lies,
Too bright for our infirm delight
The truth's superb surprise;

As lightning to the children eased
With explanation kind,
The truth must dazzle gradually
Or every man be blind.

104

After a hundred years
Nobody knows the place,—
Agony, that enacted there,
Motionless as peace.

Weeds triumphant ranged,
Strangers strolled and spelled
At the lone orthography
Of the elder dead.

Winds of summer fields
Recollect the way,—
Instinct picking up the key
Dropped by memory.

105

Through what transports of patience
I reached the stolid bliss
To breathe my blank without thee,
Attest me this and this.

By that bleak exultation
I won as near as this
Thy privilege of dying—
Abbreviate me this.

106

The life we have is very great;
The life that we shall see
Surpasses it we know because
It is infinity.

But when all space has been beheld
And all dominion shown,
The smallest human heart's extent
Reduces it to none.

Alone and in a circumstance
Reluctant to be told,
A spider on my reticence
Deliberately crawled,

And so much more at home than I
Immediately grew,
I felt myself the visitor
And hurriedly withdrew.

Revisiting my late abode
With articles of claim,
I found it quietly assumed
As a gymnasium

Where, tax asleep and title off,
The inmates of the air
Perpetual presumption took
As each were lawful heir.

If any strike me on the street
I can return the blow;
If any seize my property,
According to the law

The statute is my learnéd friend;
But what redress can be
For an offense nor here nor there,
So not in equity,

That larceny of time and mind,
The marrow of the day,
By spider—or forbid it, Lord,
That I should specify.

110

Immortal is an ample word
   When what we need is by,
But when it leaves us for a time,
   'Tis a necessity.

Of heaven above the firmest proof
   We fundamental know,
Except for its marauding hand,
   It had been heaven below.

111

like March, his shoes are purple,
   w and high;
   d for dog and peddler,
   rest dry;
   r's tongue his coming,

108

Step lightly on this narrow spot!
The broadest land that grows
Be not so ample as the breast
These emerald seams enclose.

Step lofty; for this name is told
As far as cannon dwell,
Or flag subsist, or fame export
Her deathless syllable.

109

The pungent atom in the air
Admits of no debate.
All that is named of summer days
Relinquished our estate

For what department of delight
As positive
As limit
Or

108

Step lightly on this narrow spot!
The broadest land that grows
Be not so ample as the breast
These emerald seams enclose.

Step lofty; for this name is told
As far as cannon dwell,
Or flag subsist, or fame export
Her deathless syllable.

109

The pungent atom in the air
Admits of no debate.
All that is named of summer days
Relinquished our estate —

For what depart___
As positive ___ we
As limi___ of do___inion
Or ___ dams of ecstasy.

Immortal is an ample word
   When what we need is by,
But when it leaves us for a time,
   'Tis a necessity.

Of heaven above the firmest proof
   We fundamental know,
Except for its marauding hand,
   It had been heaven below.

111

We like March, his shoes are purple,
   He is new and high;
Makes he mud for dog and peddler,
   Makes he forest dry;
Knows the adder's tongue his coming,
   And begets her close and n___
Stands the sun so ___ re hot.
   That our minds a___ ___ers;
News is he of all the ot___
   Bold it were to die
With the blue-birds buccanee___ ring
   On his British sky.

112

Who goes to dine must take his feast
Or find the banquet mean;
The table is not laid without
Till it is laid within.

For pattern is the mind bestowed
That, imitating her,
Our most ignoble services
Exhibit worthier.

113

I

Like trains of cars on tracks of plush *
I hear the level bee:
A jar across the flowers goes,
Their velvet masonry

Withstands until the sweet assault
Their chivalry consumes,
While he, victorious, tilts away
To vanquish other blooms.

II

His feet are shod with gauze,
His helmet is of gold;
His breast, a single onyx
With chrysoprase inlaid.

His labor is a chant,
His idleness a tune;
Oh, for a bee's experience
Of clovers and of noon!

114

It came at last, but prompter death
Had occupied the house,
His pallid furniture arranged
And his metallic peace.

Oh, faithful frost that kept the date!
Had love as punctual been,
Delight had aggrandized the gate
And blocked the coming in.

115

Somewhere upon the general earth
Itself exist today—
The magic, passive but extant,
That consecrated me.

Indifferent seasons doubtless play
Where I, for right to be,
Would pawn each atom that I am
But immortality,

Reserving that but just to prove
Another date of thee.
Oh, God of width, do not for us
Curtail eternity!

116

Had I not seen the sun
I could have borne the shade;
But light a newer wilderness
My wilderness has made.

117

The lilac is an ancient shrub,
But ancienter than that
The firmamental lilac
Upon the hill tonight.

The sun subsiding on his course
Bequeathes this final plant
To contemplation—not to touch—
The flower of occident.

Of one corolla is the west,
The calyx is the earth,
The capsule's burnished seeds, the stars.
The scientist of faith

His research has but just begun;
Above his synthesis
The flora unimpeachable
To time's analysis.

"Eye hath not seen" may possibly
Be current with the blind,
But let not revelation
By theses be detained.

Because that you are going
And never coming back
And I, however accurate,
May overlook your track,

Because that death is final,
However first it be,
This instant be suspended
Above mortality.

Significance that each has lived
The other to detect—
Discovery not God Himself
Could now annihilate.

Eternity, presumption,
The instant I perceive
That you, who were existence,
Yourself forgot to live.

The "life that is" will then have been
A thing I never knew,
As paradise fictitious
Until the realm of you.

The "life that is to be" to me
A residence too plain
Unless in my Redeemer's face
I recognize your own.

Of immortality who doubts
He may exchange with me,
Curtailed by your obscuring face
Of everything but he.

Of heaven and hell I also yield
The right to reprehend

To whoso would commute this face
For his less priceless friend.

If "God is love" as He admits,
We think that He must be
Because He is a jealous God
He tells us certainly.

If "all is possible" with Him
As He besides concedes,
He will refund us finally
Our confiscated gods.

119

Is Heaven a physician?
    They say that He can heal;
But medicine posthumous
    Is unavailable.

Is Heaven an exchequer?
    They speak of what we owe;
But that negotiation
    I'm not a party to.

120

September's baccalaureate
A combination is
Of crickets, crows, and retrospects,
And a dissembling breeze

That hints, without assuming,
An innuendo sere
That makes the heart put up its fun
And turn philosopher.

121

The spider as an artist
    Has never been employed
Though his surpassing merit
    Is freely certified

By every broom and Bridget
    Throughout a Christian land.
Neglected son of genius,
    I take thee by the hand.

122

'Twas later when the summer went
Than when the cricket came,
And yet we knew that gentle clock
Meant nought but going home.

'Twas sooner when the cricket went
Than when the winter came,
Yet that pathetic pendulum
Keeps esoteric time.

123

While we were fearing it, it came—
But came with less of fear
Because the fearing it so long
Had made it almost fair.

There is a fitting, a dismay—
A fitting, a despair—
'Tis harder knowing it is due
Than knowing it is here.

The trying on the utmost
The morning it is new
Is terribler than wearing it
A whole existence through.

124

The mountains stood in haze,
The valleys stopped below,
And went or waited as they liked
The river and the sky.

At leisure was the sun,
His interests of fire
A little from remark withdrawn.
The twilight spoke the spire.

So soft upon the scene
The act of evening fell
We felt how neighborly a thing
Was the invisible.

125

I thought that nature was enough
Till human nature came,
But that the other did absorb
As firmament a flame.

Of human nature just aware
There added the divine
Brief struggle for capacity.
The power to contain

Is always as the contents,
But give a giant room
And you will lodge a giant
And not a lesser man.

Until the desert knows
That water grows
His sands suffice;
But let him once suspect
That Caspian fact,
Sahara dies.

Utmost is relative,
Have not or have
Adjacent sums;
Enough, the first abode
On the familiar road
Galloped in dreams.

127

The mushroom is the elf of plants,
At evening it is not;
At morning in a truffled hut
It stops upon a spot

As if it tarried always;
And yet its whole career
Is shorter than a snake's delay,
And fleeter than a tare.

'Tis vegetation's juggler,
The germ of alibi;
Doth like a bubble antedate,
And like a bubble hie.

I feel as if the grass were pleased
To have it intermit;
The surreptitious scion
Of summer's circumspect.

Had nature any outcast face,
Could she a son contemn,
Had nature an Iscariot,
That mushroom,—it is him.

128

The Infinite a sudden guest
Has been assumed to be,
But how can that stupendous come
Which never went away?

129

Winter is good, his hoar delights
Italic flavor yield
To intellects inebriate
With summer or the world;

Generic as a quarry,
And hearty as a rose,
Invited with asperity,
But welcome when he goes.

130

Knock with tremor; these are Caesars.
Should they be at home,
Flee as if you trod unthinking
On the foot of doom.

These seceded from your substance
Centuries ago;
Should they rend you with "How are you?"
What have you to show?

131

Wonder is not precisely knowing,
And not precisely knowing not,
A beautiful but bleak condition
He has not lived who has not felt.

Suspense is his maturer sister;
Whether adult delight is pain
Or of itself a new misgiving—
This is the gnat that mangles men.

132

Lift it, with the feathers
Not alone we fly!
Launch it, the aquatic
Not the only sea!

Advocate the azure
To the lower eyes;
He has obligation
Who has paradise.

133

The rat is the concisest tenant.
He pays no rent,
Repudiates the obligation
On schemes intent

Balking our wit
To sound or circumvent.
Hate cannot harm
A foe so reticent—
Neither decree prohibit him—
Lawful as equilibrium.

134

How know it from a summer's day? *
Its fervors are as firm,
And nothing in the countenance
But scintillates the same.

Yet birds examine it and flee
And vans without a name
Inspect the admonition,
And sunder as they came.

135

The sun is one, and on the tare
He doth as punctual call
As on the conscientious flower,
And estimates them all.

136

His mansion in the pool
The frog forsakes.
He rises on a log
And statements makes.

His auditors two worlds
Deducting me,
The orator of April
Is hoarse today.

His mittens at his feet
No hand hath he,
His eloquence a bubble
As fame should be.

Applaud him, to discover
To your chagrin
Demosthenes has vanished
In forums green.

137

How much the present moment means
To those who've nothing more—
The dog, the tramp, the atheist,
Stake an entire store

Upon a moment's shallow rim,
While their commuted feet
The torrents of eternity
Do all but inundate.

138

Praise it—'tis dead, it cannot glow—
Warm this inclement ear
With the encomium it earned
Since it was gathered here.

Invest this alabaster zest
In the delights of dust
Remitted, since it flitted it,
In recusance august.

139

She laid her docile crescent down
    And this confiding stone
Still states, to dates that have forgot,
    The news that she is gone.

So constant to its stolid trust,
    The shaft that never knew,
It shames the constancy that fled
    Before its emblem flew.

140

I have no life but this,
To lead it here;
Nor any death, but lest
Dispelled from there;

Nor tie to earths to come,
Nor action new,
Except through this extent,
The realm of you.

141

Of Paradise' existence
All we know
Is the uncertain certainty,
But its vicinity infer
By its bisecting
Messenger.

142

It was a quiet seeming day,
There was no harm in earth or sky
Till with the setting sun
There strayed an accidental red,
A strolling hue one would have said,
To westward of the town.

But when the earth began to jar
And houses vanished with a roar
And human nature hid,
We comprehended by the awe,
As those that dissolution saw,
The warrant in the cloud.

143

Water makes many beds *
For those averse to sleep—
Its awful chamber open stands,
Its curtains blandly sweep.

Abhorrent is the rest
In undulating rooms
Whose amplitude no end invades,
Whose axis never comes.

144

Go not too near a House of Rose—
The depredation of a Breeze
Or inundation of a Dew
Alarm its walls away—
Nor try to tie the Butterfly,
Nor climb the Bars of Ecstasy,
In insecurity to lie
Is Joy's insuring quality.

145

The road was lit with moon and star,
The trees were bright and still;
Descried I in the distant light
A traveller on a hill

To magic perpendiculars
Ascending, though terrene,
Unknown his shimmering ultimate,
But he indorsed the sheen.

146

A route of evanescence
With a revolving wheel;
A resonance of emerald,
A rush of cochineal;
And every blossom on the bush
Adjusts its tumbled head,—
The mail from Tunis, probably,
An easy morning's ride.

147

Before you thought of spring,
Except as a surmise,
You see, God bless his suddenness,
A fellow in the skies
Of independent hues,
A little weather-worn,
Inspiriting habiliments
Of indigo and brown.

With specimens of song,
As if for you to choose,
Discretion in the interval,
With gay delays he goes
To some superior tree
Without a single leaf,
And shouts for joy to nobody
But his seraphic self!

148

One of the ones that Midas touched,
Who failed to touch us all,
Was that confiding prodigal,
The blissful oriole.

So drunk, he disavows it
With badinage divine;
So dazzling, we mistake him
For an alighting mine.

A pleader, a dissembler,
An epicure, a thief,—
Betimes an oratorio,
An ecstasy in chief;

The Jesuit of orchards,
He cheats as he enchants
Of an entire attar
For his decamping wants.

The splendor of a Burmah,
The meteor of birds,
Departing like a pageant
Of ballads and of bards.

I never thought that Jason sought
For any golden fleece;
But then I am a rural man,
With thoughts that make for peace.

But if there were a Jason,
Tradition suffer me
Behold his lost emolument
Upon the apple-tree.

149

Their barricade against the sky
The martial trees withdraw,
And with a flag at every turn
Their armies are no more.

What russet halts in nature's march
They indicate or cause,
An inference of Mexico
Effaces the surmise.

Recurrent to the after mind
That massacre of air,
The wound that was not wound nor scar,
But holidays of war.

150

Estranged from beauty none can be
For beauty is infinity,
And power to be finite ceased
When fate incorporated us.

151

'Tis whiter than an Indian pipe,
    'Tis dimmer than a lace;
No stature has it, like a fog,
    When you approach the place.

Not any voice denotes it here,
    Or intimates it there;
A spirit, how doth it accost?
    What customs hath the air?

This limitless hyperbole
    Each one of us shall be;
'Tis drama, if (hypothesis)
    It be not tragedy!

152

Glass was the street, in tinsel peril
Tree and traveller stood;
Filled was the air with merry venture,
Hearty with boys the road;

Shot the lithe sleds like shod vibrations
Emphasized and gone—
It is the past's supreme italic
Makes the present mean.

153

You cannot make remembrance grow
When it has lost its root.
The tightening the soil around
And setting it upright

Deceives perhaps the universe
But not retrieves the plant;
Real memory, like cedar feet,
Is shod with adamant.

Nor can you cut remembrance down
When it shall once have grown,
Its iron buds will sprout anew
However overthrown.

154

How happy is the little stone
That rambles in the road alone,
And doesn't care about careers,
And exigencies never fears;
Whose coat of elemental brown
A passing universe put on;
And independent as the sun,
Associates or glows alone,
Fulfilling absolute decree
In casual simplicity.

His oriental heresies
Exhilarate the bee,
And filling all the earth and air
With gay apostasy,

Fatigued at last, a clover plain
Allures his jaded eye,
That lowly breast where butterflies
Have felt it meet to die.

Intoxicated with the peace
Surpassing revelry,
He spends the evening of his days
In luscious revery,

Recounting nectars he has known
And attars that have failed,
And honeys, if his life be spared,
He hungers to attain.

156

On that specific pillow
Our projects flit away,
The night's tremendous morrow,
And whether sleep will stay

Or usher us, a stranger,
To comprehension new,
The effort to comprise it
Is all the soul can do.

157

As imperceptibly as grief
The summer lapsed away,—
Too imperceptible, at last,
To seem like perfidy.

A quietness distilled,
As twilight long begun,
Or Nature, spending with herself
Sequestered afternoon.

The dusk drew earlier in,
The morning foreign shone,—
A courteous, yet harrowing grace,
As guest who would be gone.

And thus, without a wing,
Or service of a keel,
Our summer made her light escape
Into the beautiful.

158

Hope is a subtle glutton;
    He feeds upon the fair;
And yet, inspected closely,
    What abstinence is there!

His is the halcyon table
    That never seats but one,
And whatsoever is consumed
    The same amounts remain.

159

Meeting by accident,
We hovered by design.
As often as a century
An error so divine

Is ratified by destiny;
But destiny is old
And economical of bliss
As Midas is of gold.

160

No brigadier throughout the year
So civic as the Jay.
A neighbor and a warrior too,
With shrill felicity

Pursuing winds that censure us
A February day,
The brother of the universe
Was never blown away.

The snow and he are intimate;
I've often seen them play
When heaven looked upon us all
With such severity,

I felt apology were due
To an insulted sky,
Whose pompous frown was nutriment
To their temerity.

The pillow of this daring head
Is pungent evergreens;
His larder—terse and militant—
Unknown, refreshing things;

His character is tonic,
His future a dispute;
Unfair an immortality
That leaves this neighbor out.

The bat is dun with wrinkled wings
   Like fallow article,
And not a song pervades his lips,
   Or none perceptible.

His small umbrella, quaintly halved,
   Describing in the air
An arc alike inscrutable,—
   Elate philosopher!

Deputed from what firmament
   Of what astute abode,
Empowered with what malevolence
   Auspiciously withheld.

To his adroit Creator
   Ascribe no less the praise;
Beneficent, believe me,
   His eccentricities.

162

There came a wind like a bugle;
It quivered through the grass,
And a green chill upon the heat
So ominous did pass
We barred the windows and the doors
As from an emerald ghost;
The doom's electric moccasin
That very instant passed.
On a strange mob of painting trees,
And fences fled away,

And rivers where the houses ran
The living looked that day.
The bell within the steeple wild
The flying tidings whirled.
How much can come
And much can go,
And yet abide the world!

163

Not knowing when the dawn will come
  I open every door;
Or has it feathers like a bird,
  Or billows like a shore?

164

Apparently with no surprise
To any happy flower,
The frost beheads it at its play
In accidental power.

The blond assassin passes on,
The sun proceeds unmoved
To measure off another day
For an approving God.

165

As from the earth the light balloon
Asks nothing but release—
Ascension that for which it was,
Its soaring residence—

The spirit turns upon the dust
That fastened it so long
With indignation, as a bird
Defrauded of its song.

166

Oh, Future! Thou secreted peace
Or subterranean woe,
Is there no wandering route of grace
That leads away from thee—

No circuit sage of all the course
Descried by cunning men,
To balk thee of the innocence
Advancing to thy den?

167

Death is like the insect
   Menacing the tree,
Competent to kill it,
   But decoyed may be.

Bait it with the balsam,
   Seek it with the knife,
Baffle, if it cost you
   Everything in life.

Then, if it have burrowed
   Out of reach of skill,
Ring the tree and leave it,—
   'Tis the vermin's will.

168

My life closed twice before its close;
    It yet remains to see
If Immortality unveil
    A third event to me,

So huge, so hopeless to conceive,
    As these that twice befell.
Parting is all we know of heaven,
    And all we need of hell.

169

One crown not any seek,
And yet the highest head
Its isolation coveted,
Its stigma deified.

While Pontius Pilate lives,
In whatsoever hell,
That coronation pierces him.
He recollects it well.

170

That it will never come again
Is what makes life so sweet.
Believing what we don't believe
Does not exhilarate.

That if it be, it be at best
An ablative estate,
This instigates an appetite
Precisely opposite.

171

The distance that the dead have gone
　Does not at first appear;
Their coming back seems possible
　For many an ardent year.

And then, that we have followed them
　We more than half suspect,
So intimate have we become
　With their dear retrospect.

172

'Twas here my summer paused,
What ripeness after then
To other scene or other soul?
My sentence had begun,

To winter to remove,
With winter to abide.
Go manacle your icicle
Against your tropic bride!

173

Elysium is as far as to
The very nearest room,
If in that room a friend await
Felicity or doom.

What fortitude the soul contains,
That it can so endure
The accent of a coming foot,
The opening of a door!

Notes

Texts of the poems follow those (now out of copyright) published in *The Poems of Emily Dickinson* (1937), edited by Martha Dickinson Bianchi and Alfred Leete Hampson, and those published in *Bolts of Melody* (1945), edited by Mabel Loomis Todd and Millicent Todd Bingham. Exceptions are those instances where comparison with the original texts in *The Poems of Emily Dickinson* (1955), show abrogations of meaning or felicity. In these cases—poems numbered 22, 61, 123, 133, 139, as well as poem number 97, not previously published—the texts follow those published in the Johnson edition. Other poems based on the variorum texts of Johnson are numbered 14 and 33. In all instances of texts following those in the Johnson edition, capitalization and punctuation have been regularized.

Poem 8: As recorded in *John,* III, 4, Nicodemus asked Jesus how regeneration was possible: Nicodemus saith unto him, How can a man be born when he is old? can he enter the second time into his mother's womb, and be born?

Poem 34: Follows alterations of Johnson: *ought* for *aught; steady* for *stead; infinites* for *infinite; nought* for *naught.*

Poem 48: The text follows Johnson except for the substitution of *analytic* for *narrow, probing* as suggested by Emily Dickinson.

Poem 63: The text follows Johnson except for the substitutions of *measureless* for *neighboring* and *magnify* for *multiply* in lines 4 and 8, respectively, as suggested by Emily Dickinson.

Poem 113: The text, as taken from the Bianchi edition, is actually made up of two separate poems of eight lines each. The first was written in 1872 and the second about 1864. The present text follows Bianchi except for the separation of the poem into two distinct units.

Poem 134: The text follows Johnson except for division into quatrains.

Poem 143: The text follows Johnson except for division into quatrains.

Index of First Lines

*The first number is the poem number;
the second is the page number.*

159